do you remember the color BLUE?

do you remember the color BLUE?

AND OTHER QUESTIONS KIDS ASK ABOUT BLINDNESS

by Sally Hobart Alexander

PUFFIN BOOKS

Photographic Sources

Photographs on pages 12, 25, 34, 35, 37, 38, 39, 47, 49, 52, 55, 56, 57, 61, 64, 65, 66, 68, 69, and 70 are snapshots taken from Sally Hobart Alexander's photo albums and from those of her friends and relatives. Pages 20, 21, and 45 bottom, are of tools for the visually impaired supplied generously by Sally Hobart Alexander, and were photographed by Bruce Katz. Pages 17, 45 top, 48, 50, and 53 are also tools for the visually impaired, supplied generously by Lighthouse International, and also photographed by Bruce Katz. Page 14 comes from a chart supplied generously by Dr. Richard Kavner and was photographed by Bruce Katz. The photos on pages 16 and 19 were supplied generously by Pittsburgh Vision Services. Page 29 was photographed by George Ancona and originally appeared in the book *Mom's Best Friend*, by Sally Hobart Alexander, Macmillan, 1992. Page 62 of the students from Emerson Elementary School in Parkersburg, West Virginia, was generously supplied by Lois Meadows. Page 41 of the children from the Pennsylvania School for the Deaf was generously supplied by Rosemary Gerrity. The painting on page 58 was generously supplied by Bill Irwin.

PUFFIN BOOKS
Published by the Penguin Group
Penguin Putnam Books for Young Readers,
345 Hudson Street, New York, New York 10014, U.S.A.
Penguin Books Ltd, 27 Wrights Lane, London W8 5TZ, England
Penguin Books Australia Ltd, Ringwood, Victoria, Australia
Penguin Books Canada Ltd, 10 Alcorn Avenue, Toronto, Ontario, Canada M4V 3B2
Penguin Books (N.Z.) Ltd, 182-190 Wairau Road, Auckland 10, New Zealand

Penguin Books Ltd, Registered Offices: Harmondsworth, Middlesex, England

First published in the United States of America by Viking, a division of Penguin Putnam Books for Young Readers, 2000
Published by Puffin Books, a division of Penguin Putnam Books for Young Readers, 2002

1 3 5 7 9 10 8 6 4 2

THE LIBRARY OF CONGRESS HAS CATALOGED THE VIKING EDITION AS FOLLOWS:
Alexander, Sally Hobart.
Do you remember the color blue? : and other questions kids ask about blindness / Sally Hobart Alexander.   p.   cm.
Summary: Children ask questions of an author who lost her vision at the age of twenty-six, including
"How did you become blind?" "How can you read?" and "Was it hard to be a parent when you couldn't see your kids?"
ISBN 0-670-88043-4
1. Blind Juvenile literature. 2. Blindness Juvenile literature. 3. Blind authors Biography
Juvenile literature. 4. Alexander, Sally Hobart Juvenile literature. 5. Children's questions and answers.
[1. Blind. 2. Physically handicapped. 3. Alexander, Sally Hobart. 4. Questions and answers.] I. Title.
HV1598.A38 2000 305.9'08161—dc21 99-34130 CIP

Puffin Books ISBN 0-14-230080-2

Printed in Hong Kong

To Larry, Barbara, Jack, and Lyn,
with best wishes to Peter Wallen.

contents

keep asking QUESTIONS

introduction

One day when I was walking with my cane, I overheard a little girl ask her mother, "Why is that lady holding a stick?" She was talking about me. But before I could answer her, the mother shushed her daughter and hurried away.

If I'd been able to talk to the girl, I could have told her that I was blind and the "stick," my cane, acted like a long arm, finding things I couldn't see that might trip me. That information would have answered her question and made her feel comfortable around blind people. Instead, the girl's mother made her feel that she'd done something wrong by asking.

When parents are embarrassed by their children's questions, they make kids feel that being honest is rude.

Adults seldom ask me the kinds of personal questions kids ask. Sometime after childhood, people seem to rein in their curiosity—they worry that their questions might embarrass someone, hurt him, or remind him that something is wrong.

And sometimes these questions *do* anger people. When my son was six years old, he asked a man in a wheelchair, "Will your legs ever work again?" He asked out of concern, politely and respectfully. Still, his question offended the man.

I am not insulted by straightforward questions. I prefer honesty and curiosity to silence—but not everyone feels the same. Yet I still recommend asking your question. Try beginning with a phrase like, "I hope you won't think I'm rude," or "You may not want to talk about this." Then ask the question. This way you've been perfectly polite.

When I make a school appearance to talk about my books, I'm bombarded with questions. "How do you cook and clean and match your clothes?" elementary school students ask. Practical problems interest them. Middle school kids ask about the physical aspects of being blind. "Do your eyes still blink? Do they tear? What does blindness look like? Do you remember the color blue?" High school students ask more complicated questions. "I'm not blind, but sometimes I get really down. Do you ever lose hope?"

These conversations make school visits fun and one of the best aspects of being a writer. It's because of the honest questions that come from people like you (some of the same questions you'll find answered in this book), that I dedicate the book to you.

how did you become BLIND?

Some people become blind overnight, but I lost my sight gradually over a period of two years, between the ages of twenty-four and twenty-six. I still remember everything about the day it began.

It was an ordinary day, and I was doing an ordinary thing, walking on the beach in California. The temperature was eighty degrees, even though it was November, and I dove into the water and swam. After a while, I turned onto my back and floated, staring at the blue sky. That's when I saw a tiny black line, the size of an eyelash. The line moved up and down, then wiggled like a snake on the water's surface. I swam back to the beach, and had walked a few feet, when the line disappeared. I didn't know it then, but that small line would alter the whole course of my life.

I wasn't too worried at that moment. But because I'd just started wearing contact lenses, I decided to see my doctor. He told me I had a simple infection and gave me eyedrops, and I went back to teaching without giving my eyes another thought—until the line showed up again two months later. It branched and rebranched into a bush, then disappeared altogether. But this time my sight disappeared with it. All I could see out of my right eye was a dense fog. My stomach and everything inside me grew tight. I tested and retested my eye, hoping the fog would go away, but it didn't for three days.

Weeks of hospitalization, of bed rest, of eye patches followed.

11

Weeks and months of uncertainty, of fear, of dependency I raged against. Months of acting brave when I really wanted to scream or cry or run away. But I couldn't run away. I was trapped in a body going haywire.

All I learned from the tests and the doctor visits was that blood vessels inside the retina of my right eye were breaking. I didn't seem to have any disease at all.

Think for a minute. You break blood vessels every day. You scrape your elbow or knee, and it bleeds. You wash the scrape, maybe put on medicine and a bandage. No big deal. But when blood vessels break inside your eye, it is a big deal. The inside of the eye contains a crystal clear liquid. Even the tiniest drop of blood turns the liquid murky and clouds your vision. The drop of blood can scar the retina, and enough scarring causes blindness.

Sally, 1968

In those first months, my only hope was that my left eye would stay healthy. But that eye started to bleed, too. One eye would always be clear enough for me to function, but each hemorrhage caused more damage. Each took away more sight.

12

Such a tiny set of cells, such a small portion of my body, was shattering my life, my whole identity, and I couldn't do anything to stop it.

At the urging of my parents, I went back to Pennsylvania and saw my childhood ophthalmologist. He was a family friend and spoke honestly to me. I would never get back the sight I'd lost, he told me, and if the hemorrhaging didn't stop, I'd be blind. Every detail of that appointment is still vivid in my memory—the doctor's sad expression, the heat in the room, the enormous effort I made to keep control.

I spent the rest of that day fighting tears. What would I do with myself? What kind of life could I have?

That same evening we went out to celebrate my brother-in-law's birthday. The conversation centered around upcoming family weddings, and I wondered if anyone would want to marry me now. Back home, I rushed inside, wanting the privacy of my old bedroom. But I didn't get that far. I found my brother in the living room waiting to surprise us. I ran to him. "I'm going to be blind, Bobby. I'm going to be blind." I cried until my head hammered with pain.

The next few months were a kind of limbo. I went to doctor after doctor, never learning anything new. At this point, my right eye was much more damaged than my left. I couldn't read or see much detail out of it. But though affected, my left eye was still intact enough for reading, for driving, for most things. Until three days before my brother's wedding.

My sister and I were walking to the final fitting of our bridesmaid's dresses, when I saw a dark pool spill on the sidewalk. I stopped walking. But the black pool wasn't outside; it was inside my eye—my good eye. My left retina had detached—pulled away from the back of my eye.

That evening I arrived at the hospital in New York City to learn that

13

my surgery would be on the day of my brother's rehearsal dinner, so I'd miss his wedding. Even worse news was that the doctor didn't think he'd be able to reattach my retina. Right then, I could see light and nothing more. If this operation didn't work, I'd be totally blind.

Despite my doctor's fear, the surgery was a success. I regained sight in the bottom half of my eye, so that I could make out the legs of furniture, steps, curbs, anything on ground level. Still, I couldn't read print, and was now considered legally blind. (A person is considered legally blind when he sees at twenty feet, with the strongest lenses, what someone with perfect vision sees at two hundred feet [20/200 vision]). My

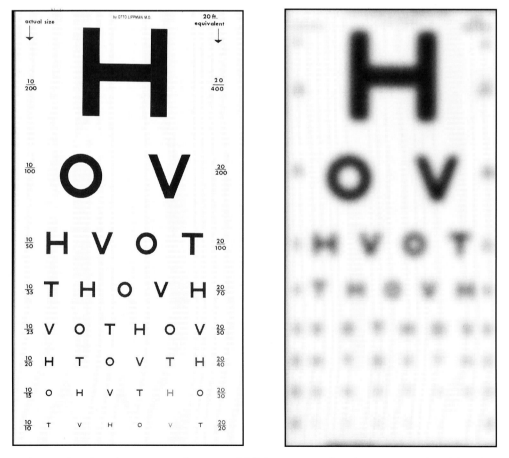

Eye charts showing the contrast between 20/20 vision and 20/200 vision—legal blindness

life was changed forever. Legal blindness wasn't one loss; it was many. I could no longer read or write, find my clothes, eat, cook, walk outside, teach, or do any of the things I'd done independently my whole life. Blindness turned me from an adult back to a child, needing help from my family again. And I didn't want that.

Within a month I found a training program in Pittsburgh for newly blind adults. When I finished the program fifteen weeks later, I felt as if I were beginning a whole new life. I accepted a teaching job in the same program, and for the first time since my eye problems began, life took on a routine. I had one setback on the day before Thanksgiving 1969, when blood vessels broke in my left eye and destroyed the rest of my sight. Any bit of vision is helpful, so this final loss shook my confidence. Once again, the world looked different. But I took more cane lessons to sharpen my skills, and soon I was back on track, moving forward through this new way of life.

was it SCARY at first?

When I was little, I was afraid of the dark. I just knew that all kinds of scary things were lurking, waiting to reach out and grab me. So before I went to sleep, I made my father look under the bed, in my closet, and in every drawer of my dresser to make sure nothing was hiding there. I don't remember when this fear went away, but when I found out that I was going blind, the terror came back. I thought blind people lived in blackness, and I dreaded that fate.

But I was wrong. When I became totally blind, my world didn't go jet black or even shadowy. With my eyes open or closed, I saw a smoky white fog.

Even though I didn't have to be afraid of living in darkness, I still found other things to worry about: bumping myself, breaking a bone, falling down steps, being hit by a car. Most of all, I worried about making mistakes and embarrassing myself. I thought the training program—which was a residential program that took fifteen weeks—would help me deal with all these fears.

Yet on that first day at the Greater Pittsburgh Guild for the Blind, I was as terrified as any kid facing the first day of school.

A classmate of Sally's at the Greater Pittsburgh Guild for the Blind, April 1969

16

Picture a raw, drizzly April afternoon, a lobby filled with plastic chairs on an ugly green tile floor. Picture me, barely able to see out of the bottom of my left eye, sitting next to someone rocking back and forth so hard I could feel a breeze. At the same time, someone else walked past with her arms out like tentacles. I wanted to run out the door and go home. Instead, I just kept to myself, spending my free time those first few days sleeping. After the third day, I got so bored I decided to give the other trainees a chance. By the end of the training, fifteen weeks later, I actually felt comfortable with—even close to—the very people I'd thought were so strange.

When I encountered more difficult tasks in the training I still felt scared sometimes, but in that first week my classes took so much attention I didn't have enough room in my mind for worrying. Especially in the cane training class.

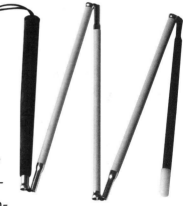

Learning to handle a cane was as complicated as learning to swing a baseball bat. So many things to remember at once. "Touch, don't tap," my instructor said. Easier said than done. Once I learned to coordinate my feet and cane, I moved outside with speeding cars, rushing pedestrians—even open manholes. To make matters worse, my teacher made me wear goggles that covered up the little bit of

A fold-up cane

sight I still had. The goggles forced me to rely only on what I heard and felt to get around. During those first steps outside, my legs were weak, my hands, shaky. Yet in a few days, I learned to feel grates, ups, downs, and carpeting; to hear swishing revolving doors and overhanging roofs and movie marquees that echoed my footsteps. I learned how to cross streets, how to function in busy downtown areas, how to take buses, and much more.

Although every class taught us how to survive, two classes, in particular—visualization and sensory training—interested me.

Visualization was a class only for people like me, who had been able to see before. This class taught me to exercise my visual memory. If I could picture things, I'd be able to memorize the layouts of buildings and neighborhoods.

With time, memories fade, except for the really emotional ones. All of us retain muscle memories—how to ride a bike, for example—longer than we keep visual memories. Worse yet, when we go blind, the part of the brain that allows seeing isn't stimulated. But the part of the brain that allows visualizing, the parietal lobe, can still be stimulated. By picturing things, we can retrieve memories.

In class I practiced visualizing colors, everyday objects, nature scenes, city streets. My teacher couldn't predict how long I'd keep the ability to visualize. It varies with each person and depends on experience and what we've stored up. When I was a little girl, I always made up movies in my head. As a writer, I visualize the scenes in my books. Using that skill, exercising my brain, I've been able to keep my visual memory for thirty years.

I exercised my other senses in sensory training class by identifying objects we touched, smelled, and tasted, and by identifying sounds we heard. Vision is ordinarily dominant in people. Like a bossy older brother or sister, it takes over even when you don't mean it to. When a friend calls you on the phone, for example, you don't have to ask who it is because you recognize her voice. Yet when the same friend calls your name at school, you turn and look in order to identify her. You've been trained to trust your eyes more than your ears. In the same way, vision also dominates smell, touch, and taste.

Vision helps people take in the world from a distance. Smell, touch, and taste are more intimate. They force us to observe the world close up.

Contrary to what most people think, when one sense is missing, the rest don't grow stronger. Instead, since I had fewer senses competing for my attention, I learned to focus more on hearing, smell, touch, and taste. I had to use my other senses—to trust them. Like an athlete training his muscles, I exercised those senses day after day to substitute for sight.

At the Guild I had other important classes—Braille, typing, hand-writing, grooming, cooking, cleaning, recreation, and counseling. The classes gave me the skills to re-enter the world as an independent adult. Knowledge doesn't only give independence, it gives courage. Just as I'd outgrown my childhood fear of the dark, I outgrew my fear of being blind and learned to walk back into the world unafraid.

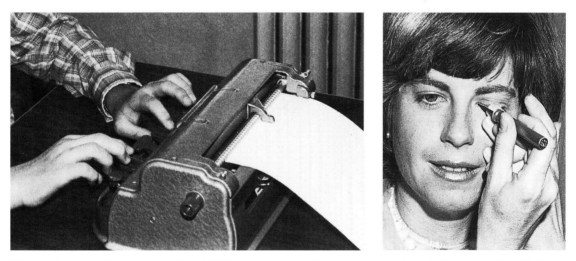

These photographs, taken in the 1960s, show how classes looked when Sally was at the Guild: they show Braille class and makeup class

helpful
tools

BRAILLE CLOTHING TAG

About the size of a fingernail, these metal tags have holes at either end for pinning or sewing onto labels. They tell me colors: "YW" for yellow, "PK" for pink, and "PP" for purple. When clothes are multicolored, I pin several tags onto the labels at once.

BRAILLE TIMER

Usually three inches high and two inches wide, this device has raised dots by each number and works just like any other timer. I also use Braille recipes and Braille labels on spices and cans. My microwave has a Braille pad.

BRAILLE WATCH

Imagine a life without clocks or watches, and you'll have an idea of my life when I first became blind. I dialed the phone number for the exact time so often I memorized it. I'd always taken telling time for granted, and I felt lost. I developed a good sense of how long it took to do things, but my estimates could be off by ten minutes. Without a watch, I could miss a bus or an appointment. I could arrive at work late.

A Braille watch saved me. It looks like a regular wristwatch, except that the crystal pops up when you push a button, usually the winder. You can feel that the hour hand is shorter and sits below the minute hand. All the numbers have raised dots beside them. The numbers 3, 6, and 9 have two raised dots, and the 12 has three.

TALKING CLOCK

These clocks come in many varieties. The most common is pocket sized, but I've had talking clocks inside ballpoint pens and keychains. You simply push a button, and a robot voice calls out the time.

21

if your EYES don't see, do they work at all?

Unlike many visually impaired people who can see the tops, middles, or bottoms of things, or at least shapes, colors, and light, I can't see anything. I can't tell day from night unless I feel the sun on my cheeks. I can't tell if a lamp is on or off unless I touch the bulb.

Although my eyes don't work for vision, they still function in other ways. For example, they feel pain. If I am poked in the eye, it hurts.

After I'd lost my sight, some friends and I were sitting in my parents' backyard near the basketball hoop. Two of them started dribbling a ball and taking a few shots.

I used to play basketball, so when they asked me to try shooting, I hopped up eagerly. One friend stood under the basket and called out, helping me find the net. I tossed the ball, and it hit the rim, bouncing away. Without thinking, my friend caught it and hurled it back to me. The ball struck me square in the face, smacking my nose and eyes. At that moment, I knew real pain.

Objects from the outside, then, can cause my eyes pain. That's because the cornea has more pain-sensing nerves than any other organ in the body. Just like a crystal on a watch, the cornea is the actual surface of the eye and has no protection. I didn't feel pain from the bleeding on the inside of my eyes that destroyed my sight. There aren't any pain-sensing nerves in that part of the eye.

Even though I'm blind, my eyes still get sick. The retinal bleeding that caused my blindness, for instance, also led to a problem in my right eye—glaucoma. This is a painful condition created by increased pressure in the eyeball. Fortunately, the eye drops managed the pain. Years later, calcium formed on the cornea of my right eye, then flaked off, leaving a tiny open wound. Medicine helped, but the wound took several weeks to heal.

In addition to feeling pain, my eyes can also shed tears. If I dice onions or sit by a smoking bonfire, they water. If I'm sad, I cry. When something slips into my eye, my lids blink, and my eyes tear to get rid of it. And my eyes still move. They mostly move together, just the way yours do. They might stray a little, because they can't lock onto any object to keep themselves straight.

So my eyes still function, just not in the traditional way. But because they function at all, my friends ask if they could be repaired. Could I have a transplant?

A few blind people have gained sight from surgery. But recovering sight as an adult doesn't always make life much easier. Most often, the brains of people who are born blind can't understand distance and depth perception. To formerly blind people, the furniture in a room all seems to look flat—as if it's sitting in a row. Going down steps is still easier with their eyes closed, because everything they see appears two-dimensional. In this situation, touch is still preferable to sight. They *can* adjust somewhat to a three-dimensional world, but they can never catch up to someone born sighted.

And even with twenty-five years of seeing, I might run into difficulties if I recovered sight. Much of my visual functioning would be rusty after thirty blind years. I might be able to distinguish a triangle from a square right away, but it would take time to distinguish more complex shapes. A person born blind would have distance and depth perception problems, but I would have problems recognizing all the details.

So would I like to see again? You bet. If there were an operation to restore my vision, I would volunteer for it right away. But no operation is possible.

To be able to see, I would need a whole new eye. So far doctors cannot transplant an entire eye, just the cornea and other parts. To transplant an eye, doctors would have to cut the optic nerve. Once they did that, they would have to suture 1,200,000 nerves together, and that's impossible.

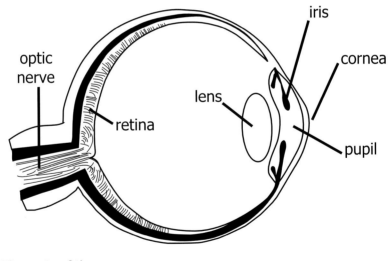

The parts of the eye

why blind people wear sunglasses

Sally with sunglasses, 1970

Eye contact is important to many people, but no totally blind person can make it, except haphazardly. Sighted people often feel uncomfortable when they talk to somebody who can't look directly at them. Sunglasses make the lack of eye contact less obvious and put sighted people at ease. Blind people also wear them for protection and for a better appearance if their eyes are visibly damaged.

Sally without sunglasses, 1970

how does your DOG work?

When I was growing up, my family always had dogs for pets, mongrels from the pound or strays from the neighborhood. Today I still have a dog, but she's not just a pet. She's my dog guide. Even though I'd used a cane for nine years, I decided to switch to a dog after my son was born. I couldn't answer his questions and still concentrate enough on the things I needed to hear and feel.

I went to the oldest training school in the country, The Seeing Eye, where Marit, a German shepherd, and I trained for three and a half weeks. We had two lessons a day on routes that grew increasingly difficult. At first, I worried they'd chosen a dog that was too speedy for me. But soon I could keep up with her and knew they'd made the perfect choice—a dog who was comfortable in the city and gentle with small children. Marit and I worked together for twelve years. She became an important part of our family. After she died, I felt lost. I missed her wonderful personality, her smell, the feel of her fur, her companionship. And I missed her help. My cane skills were rusty, so I returned to The Seeing Eye for another German shepherd, Ursula.

Although Ursula is a dog guide, when she is out of harness, she acts just like all the pets I had growing up. She races around our house in a circle through the kitchen, living room, and dining room. She is clever enough to figure out that I can't see, so she keeps quiet when she's get-

26

ting into mischief. She scrapes her bowl along the floor to let me know she's thirsty. She barks and puts her paws on the counter when she wants a treat. When she's tired, Ursula curls up under my desk, inside the fireplace, even in the shower stall. She is terrified of thunderstorms and, after being attacked by two Afghan hounds, was even afraid of other dogs for a while.

I love Ursula like a third child. Love is the basis of our training. It's the reason she fights her instincts (to romp with dogs or chase squirrels and cats) while she guides me. Part of our training included two months of being together around the clock, which created an extraordinary bond.

To keep Ursula's guiding skills sharp, I work her twice a day for about two miles, rain or sunshine, snow or ice, whether or not I have errands to run. When I strap the harness around her, she knows it's time to work. I can't tell Ursula, "McDonald's, please," and have her take me there. Ursula is not a cab driver. In the dog guide system, Ursula does half the work; I do the other half.

When I leave my house, I need to have a map inside my head of all the streets I'll cross and the turns I'll make to get to my

my job

destination. When I reach the right block, I listen or feel for clues to help me find the building I want. When I arrive at an intersection, I have to decide whether the light is green or red. Ursula can't make that decision for me. Dogs don't see the variety of colors that people do. To dogs, green, red, and yellow all look the same.

Some traffic lights beep when the light is green, but my neighborhood doesn't have any like that. Instead, I listen to the way the cars are traveling. If they're moving in front of me, I know not to step into the street. If they're moving next to me, I know the light is green, and I can cross freely.

ursula's job

Ursula guides me down sidewalks so that I don't bump into anything—garbage cans, telephone poles, low-hanging branches. She leads me around potholes or open manholes, hesitates at every street corner and every large step up or down. If there is construction or an obstacle on the sidewalk, she circles around it. If she can't make the move safely or without going into the street, she stops, to warn me. Finally, if I tell her to cross a street when a car is coming, she is trained to disobey me. Loud noises like roaring lawn mowers can drown out the sound of cars, making it difficult for me to judge correctly. Disobeying unsafe commands is a dog guide's most important job.

common commands

Forward
Right
Left
Hup up (which means go faster)
Steady (which means go slower)
Pfui (which means bad)
Come
Sit
Down
Fetch
Rest (which means stay)

dog guide history

Sally and Ursula

The idea of formally training dogs to guide blind people has been around since World War I. In Potsdam, German shepherd dogs were trained to lead blinded veterans. The concept came to the United States when a woman from Philadelphia agreed to breed German shepherds for more alertness and stamina for the Swiss army. In 1927 she wrote an article for the *Saturday Evening Post* about the dog guide school she'd seen in Germany. As a result of her article, a lot of blind people wrote asking for a dog.

One man, Morris Frank, wrote, "Train me, and I will show people here how a blind man can be absolutely on his own." Morris Frank trained with his first dog guide, Buddy, in Switzerland. Back in the United States, he traveled across the country, challenging himself and Buddy with every traffic situation, proving that a blind man could be independent. The Seeing Eye began in 1929. Since then, nine other dog training centers, each with a different name, have opened in the United States. Still, because Seeing Eye was first, many people mistakenly refer to all dog guides as Seeing Eye dogs.

a trip to the grocery store

With Ursula's leash and harness in my left hand, I say, "Forward," and walk from my house to the street. I tell Ursula, "Left." She trots along, crossing driveways and walkways, not stopping until she comes to the first cross street, Wightman Avenue.

"Ursula, left," I say again, moving my right hand in that direction. We arrive at a busy intersection. Once I decide that the light is green, we can cross.

"Ursula, forward," I say. When we step up onto the curb across the street, I give another left command. Ursula and I make a right turn at the next intersection and cross two more streets before we reach the block with the grocery store.

We continue until I sense an awning overhead. Like an overhanging roof, the awning echoes my footsteps. Just past the awning, the sidewalk rises, then falls. As soon as it levels off, I know I'm at the store.

"Ursula, right." This time Ursula knows where we are headed. She pulls eagerly to enter the store with its good smells, good spills. She still hopes for a friendly pat from the check-out clerk, but I've asked him to ignore her. Pats distract her from her work, and she might guide me into a shelf.

tales of heroic guide dogs

Morris Frank, the first dog guide user in America, once told his dog Buddy to walk into an elevator. Buddy refused. Morris had heard the elevator doors open, so he repeated the command, "Forward." Buddy still didn't move. In frustration, Morris stepped toward the elevator, but Buddy threw himself across his feet. The elevator shaft was empty. Buddy saved his owner from falling to his death.

One morning my first dog and I were walking, when all of a sudden, Marit's back end shoved into me, shoved so hard that she forced me backward. I was starting to scold her when I heard a car speeding up a driveway—straight at me. Marit kept pushing until I turned and ran with her into the empty street. The driver saw me and stopped just as the bumper of the car hit the back of my legs, knocking me forward, making me stumble. The driver sped off, never checking to see if I was okay. I wasn't hurt, just shaken up. All the way home I wondered what would have happened if I hadn't had Marit with me. A scary thought.

Our dog guides aren't trained to protect us. They're trained only to lead. But all dog users can tell stories of this kind of heroism.

how did you meet your HUSBAND, when you couldn't see him?

Strangely enough, I met my husband, Bob, on a blind date. It's even more ironic because I'd grown to hate that expression, "blind date." To me, the word *blind* meant not being able to see. Bob could see fine, so why call him that? He was my one and only "blind date"; yet, he's the one who stuck.

I'd been on dates before Bob, but things didn't work out for one reason or another. I was even engaged once, but after I learned I was going to be blind, we broke up.

The training program took too much concentration for me to think about a social life. When I finished and was living on my own, I wanted to start dating again. But meeting men wasn't easy. I didn't run into many single men—at least that I knew of. I could pass an attractive man in the grocery store and never know. Anywhere I went, I could be right next to a gorgeous movie star and have no idea.

My big chance to meet men came when a friend from college asked me to a party, but the evening proved to be a complete disaster. Imagine being blind at a huge party, and having your date leave to talk to a friend. The house is wall-to-wall strangers. How would you begin to meet people? That's the dilemma I faced at this party. In the past I'd been able to flirt, to make eye contact with someone I wanted to meet. But without a lingering look, what else could I use? A touch would be too risky, especially when I couldn't see what I was touching. And I'd already used too much cologne. If I sprayed any more on myself to attract a man, I'd cut off all the oxygen in the room.

But how could I even start a conversation? When someone finally spoke in my direction, I nearly kissed him in gratitude, then found out he was talking to somebody else. After that, I searched for something to say, but all my brilliant ideas relied on being able to compliment someone's clothes or hair, which was impossible now. I ended up saying something dumb like, "Hot in here, isn't it?" Three people answered me, thinking I was speaking to them.

I was mortified and wanted to leave, but I couldn't get away without hitting everybody with my cane. And the only person I really wanted to hit was my date.

Back home, I threw myself on the bed and cried. I hated my insensitive date, but more than that, I hated myself, this new blind self.

In the morning I talked to a friend who helped me laugh at the catastrophe the night before.

Finally, my luck changed. Someone who'd gotten my name from a mutual friend called to ask me out. We talked for a while, and he made me laugh. So far, so good. He was an English professor in Pittsburgh. But, just my luck, he called the night before our date and postponed it. He'd been invited to a party at his college and wanted to go. I was upset. Why didn't he want to take me along?

Bob arrived the next day and took my hands in his. He apologized right away. "Sorry about last night. I almost invited you, but it was a mob scene. I thought it'd be better to meet this way."

He was straightforward, and sensitive enough to know how overwhelming a crowded party would be. This was a good sign.

I picked up my cane and walked into the hall. We were going to a movie, something most dates didn't think I'd enjoy. But Bob had asked directly and learned that I still enjoyed movies, as long as they weren't full of action and special effects.

Bob closed the door behind us. "You're doing great, but let me know if I can help."

I smiled. "Maybe I'll take your arm. That will free me to talk."

His arm had a nice muscle, and, better yet, he was tall, something I required, since I was five feet ten. All the way to the movie we talked— current events, his work, my job search. Conversation came easily, and I enjoyed his dry sense of humor. Bob was terrific at describing the silent parts of the film. Nothing like an English professor, who specialized in words, to narrate. I stayed awake, not always the case at movies. We went back to my apartment for a while, then Bob left, asking to see me again.

Bob and Sally, 1974

Friends always wonder how I knew I was attracted to a man when I couldn't see. Without being able to judge appearance, I felt attracted to how a man acted, what he said and did. But often I kissed someone and realized that

I didn't feel romantically about him. That didn't happen with Bob. His goodnight kiss met all my romantic expectations.

And he was dependable. Soon after this first date, I developed glaucoma. After several months, I had such severe pain in my eye that I had to fly to a hospital in Philadelphia. Within a few hours, Bob arrived at the hospital, also by plane. I knew then I could always count on

Sally and Bob, twenty-fifth wedding anniversary, 1999

him. He was loving, hard-working, and definitely the right guy. But I didn't propose to him until months later. Now, after twenty-five years, I'm still glad he said yes.

is it hard to be a blind PARENT?

From the time Bob and I decided to marry, we looked forward to having a family. One friend thought it was a mistake, saying, "Bob will have to do all the work." He didn't think a blind person could handle diapering, feeding, bathing, and all the jobs that go with parenting. But Bob and I had already talked about the baby care and figured out how we could manage.

Another friend still didn't think it was a good idea, because our children might inherit my eye condition. We were concerned about that, too, of course, and checked with the eye doctor, who told us our children wouldn't be at risk. So we decided to go ahead and have a family.

When I had each baby—first a boy, and then a girl—I asked the doctors to let me hold my child right away.

"How are the eyes?" I asked before counting the toes or fingers or ears.

Both times I heard the answer I was waiting for—perfect.

At those births, I felt a terrible yearning to see, unlike any longing before or since. My husband saw this and took my finger, rubbing it over Joel's head.

"Your wavy hair, Sal."

When Leslie was born, he took my finger again, moving it along her chin. "Her mama's jaw," he said, "and, I think, her long legs."

I smiled. Bob knew how to shake me out of my self-pity. Besides, the sound, smell, and feel of my kids were spectacular. Sight wasn't the only way to enjoy and admire them.

From the very beginning I was sure that my children understood I was blind. Even when they were babies, they gurgled and made noise so I could find them. They learned to put my hand on objects they wanted me to "see." When they started walking and moving farther away, they made sounds over and over until I echoed them. Their doctor said that was because they needed contact with me before going any farther.

At first, my kids probably thought that all mothers were blind. As they got older and their worlds grew wider, they learned that *mother* was not a synonym for *blind*. They saw that other kids' mothers moved faster and drove cars, just like their dad.

When our son was five months old and in a baby carrier on my back, he would grab my shoulders at every intersection to warn me that we'd come to a street. Unlike their playmates, Joel and Leslie wore bells on their shoes. When Leslie grew big enough to replace her brother in the baby carrier, I wrapped a child's harness around Joel so that I could feel him walking beside us.

Sally with Leslie (back) and Joel (front), 1980

When they were old enough to play outside, I

37

Sally with Joel, 1977

placed them first in a large, wooden corral. When they grew older still, they played in our fenced-in yard with a locked gate.

Did they mind the bells, the harness, the fence? I don't think so. They were young enough that other kids were intrigued by the bells and harness and didn't tease them.

But being a blind parent has its drawbacks. Even at preschool age, my kids figured out my weak points and tested me. They slipped off their jingly shoes when they didn't want me to find them. They sneaked cookies, forgetting that I could smell the chocolate on their breath.

When they grew older, they tested me in more clever ways. At bedtime they switched the light back on to read or organize baseball cards. I knew because I found the books or cards in their covers the next morning.

Although I didn't spank often, when I really lost my temper and swung, I could never connect to any bottoms. My kids were expert dodgers. The most clever dodging of all came when our son and a friend were having a pillow fight in the living room. I was rushing downstairs when I heard the crash of our Hopi Indian pot.

"Joel!" I screamed and swatted where I thought his ten-year-old backside should be.

As I struck the target, Joel's friend yelled, "I'm not Joel!"

Right then the boy's mother arrived at my open door and witnessed my crime. Fortunately, she laughed, but I was shamed enough to give up spanking forever.

Since I can't see them, Joel and Leslie understand that I really want to hear them. I grill and probe and force out their thoughts, then talk their ears off. I also hug them a lot. I make no apology for using my sense of touch to excess. That's a blind parent's special privilege.

When Joel and Leslie were teenagers, two mistakes I made mortified them: I talked to people after they had already walked away, and I answered people who weren't speaking to me.

Think about it. If I am talking to a store clerk, I might not hear him step away. Blind people speak regularly to empty cash registers, empty chairs, empty rooms.

If I'm standing in line and the cashier says something in my direction, I have no way of knowing if she's really talking to me or to the person behind me. Without eye contact, it's impossible to figure out.

Sometimes I goof even standing alone. In a hotel lobby, a man came toward me, saying, "Oh, you're beautiful."

"Why, thank you," I replied.

"Sorry," he said, "I was talking to your dog."

When I told my kids, they said the man was just tactless. Even though I embarrass them, Joel and Leslie feel protective. It's okay if they tease and test me, but they don't want anyone else doing that.

Joel and Leslie, 1996

39

would you rather be blind or DEAF?

Several years ago I spoke to a group of kids at the Western Pennsylvania School for the Deaf. When I arrived, the librarian told me five kids were finishing up a rhythm class.

"What's that?" I asked, taking a seat nearby.

"The children learn to move and dance to the vibrations of the music. Low notes have the most vibrations. High notes have the fewest."

I listened and tried to feel the vibrations through the chair, while the teacher beat out rhythms with a drum.

"Today she's teaching them to skip," the librarian explained.

Just then, the drumbeat stopped. "They're smiling at you," their teacher told me.

I smiled back and waved, then heard a rustle from their direction.

They thundered across the floor and sat down with me.

I raised my hand and reviewed the finger spelling alphabet. When I goofed on a letter, the kids corrected me by placing my fingers in the right positions. Soon I had the alphabet down and began asking them questions.

"What is your name?" I asked with my fingers. "How old are you?"

They spelled the answers back into my hand. Next, they asked me questions.

"What's your dog's name? How old is she?"

A few minutes later, we all went on to an assembly in the auditorium, where I now had five friends in the large audience. While I spoke in my normal voice, a teacher stood beside me, interpreting everything I said in sign language.

"People always want to know if I'd rather be blind or deaf," I told them. "Are you asked that question, too?"

"All their heads are nodding," the interpreter said.

I smiled. "What do you answer?"

"Oh my," said the interpreter, laughing. "Every hand is in the air."

One by one she called on them, and they signed their responses. Every single one preferred to be deaf.

"You can't see beautiful things," one girl signed, "beautiful animals, sunsets, mountains, snowfalls, oceans."

"You can't see how handsome I am," a boy signed.

A rhythm class at the Western Pennsylvania School for the Deaf

41

At lunch I sat with a dozen teenagers. They each wanted a chance to answer the same question. All twelve preferred deafness to blindness.

"How do *you* feel?" a girl spelled into my hand.

"I'd rather be blind," I said, only finger spelling the last word.

"Good for you," she said into my hand, and I understood. Thinking my problem wasn't as bad as somebody else's showed acceptance, adjustment.

Vision *is* such a pleasure. I've often longed to see, even dreamed I could see my husband and my kids, the sights I miss most. Still, I talk to them every day. I love hearing the sound of their voices, their laughter, the funny things they say. I wouldn't ever want to give that up in order to see them.

I know a quadriplegic man who can move his arms and hands somewhat by using his shoulder muscles. He can hold a cup, bring it to his lips, and even feed himself. His greatest fear from childhood was losing his sight.

"Not seeing," he said, "would be worse than quadriplegia."

I was shocked. Could he actually believe this? Didn't I have more independence? A fuller life? But he managed to drive his own van and his own motorboat. He'd even managed to accumulate a few speeding tickets.

After talking to the kids at the School for the Deaf, I began realizing there was no consensus on which disability was better or worse. I am blind, but I still go to movies. A friend or family member describes what's happening when the actors aren't speaking. The kids at the School for the Deaf can't hear, yet they dance to vibrations they feel from the music. My friend in the wheelchair can barely move, yet he finds a way to drive.

Now that I'm blind, I read with my ears and fingers: my ears listen to books on tape, and my fingers feel Braille. But for twenty-six years, I read with my eyes.

A major milestone in the course of my blindness was losing the ability to read out of my right eye. Within two months I couldn't read out of my left eye either.

Suddenly, I couldn't read newspapers or find telephone numbers and addresses. I couldn't read notes I'd written to myself, couldn't read my journal. I couldn't manage anything written—not even the labels on cans. The results were devastating. When I ironed a blouse one day, for instance, I used furniture polish instead of spray starch. When I made lunch another day, I opened a can of condensed milk, not the soup I wanted.

But the most devastating frustration of all was not being able to read my fiancé's letters. He stopped writing, and instead, we talked on the phone. Soon our phone bills were so high we had to cut back, talk less often. I really missed the contact, especially from his letters. He communicated better in writing, expressed more feelings, and said more tender, romantic things.

But even with these frustrations, something important happened. While I lay in a hospital bed with my eyes patched, a nurse rolled a talking book machine into my room. This machine was a record player that played recordings of books. She offered me different choices: *Pride and Prejudice, The Great Gatsby,* and *Middlemarch.* I'd never read as a hobby and had barely heard of these titles, but I figured I'd give them a try. In that three-week hospital stay when I couldn't move out of bed, I made the big discovery: books. They were funny, romantic, and human, and they helped me escape from everything that was troubling me.

Back at my parents' house, I ordered talking books from the library. I "read" as I ate, as I got dressed, as I knitted. Without intending to, I fell in love with books. I became a "reader," even though I was considered blind.

Yet talking books didn't meet all my reading needs. There were hundreds of things I needed to read that weren't books. What would I do in order to read newspapers, mail, labels? How could I find telephone numbers? I learned that I needed a combination: talking books, Braille, human assistance, and new technologies.

Braille

When I became blind in 1968, I assumed that all blind people knew Braille, but I was wrong. Back then, only twenty-five percent of the visually impaired used it. Now, that figure has dropped to eight percent. One reason for the small number is the difficulty people have in learning Braille. Another reason is that the majority of blind people are elderly and have trouble feeling the dots. Younger visually impaired people often have enough sight to read

a	b	c	d	e	f	g	h	i	j	k	l	m

n	o	p	q	r	s	t	u	v	w	x	y	z

1	2	3	4	5	6	7	8	9	0

magnified or large print and are told to read with their vision, because print is easier to learn and is available everywhere. It is less bulky. Compare your print vest-pocket dictionary to my Braille one, for instance— seven volumes, each a foot high and four inches thick.

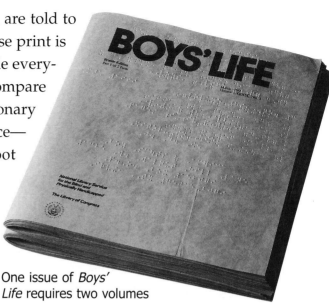

No one told me to use my vision, because I didn't have enough to read with. I'd have to learn Braille, and that would be hard. Every letter of the Braille alphabet

One issue of *Boys' Life* requires two volumes

is made up of different arrangements of six raised dots, in two equal columns, like the number six on a pair of dice. For each letter, each number, and each mark of punctuation, I had to memorize which dots went where.

Next came the completely unfamiliar part: feeling the bumps with my fingertips, figuring out where one letter ended and another began. Often, I could only determine that by scraping with my fingernail. Learning Braille was as challenging as memorizing a whole new language.

I took four months to master it. Now, I read about thirty words a minute. Some people can manage up to one hundred or more. I use Braille for recipes, telephone numbers, and addresses. I label spices (right), cans, tapes, and CDs. I make reminder lists for myself and outline

speeches and books in Braille; and I receive Braille newsletters through the mail. Even though I'm slow, Braille is crucial to my independence and keeps my spelling from deteriorating.

readers

Even with Braille and talking books, I still have mail to read. I hire teenagers for two-hour reading sessions each week. Right now, three different boys come one day a week each.

And that's not enough. My husband reads our mail, too. When my kids are home, they also have to work.

scanner

A scanner connected to my computer photographs typewritten material, then reads it out loud. This machine is a great help, but again not perfect. Some print is faded, or one letter might be darker or lighter than another. This causes the scanner to mispronounce words. If the typeface is unrecognizable or if there are illustrations, the scanner is confused.

opticon

Years ago I bought an opticon, an eight-inch square machine with two parts: a camera about the size of a thumb and a slot for my index finger. I move the camera over typewritten material and the machine translates each letter into vibrations shaped like that letter, on my fingertip. I can read five words a minute with the opticon, but after a half hour my finger loses sensitivity. Some people read up to thirty words a minute with it. They use it for reading all their bills, because numbers don't show up as well on the scanner. They also use the opticon to doublecheck what they've scanned.

Before I lost my sight, I thought that Braille met all the reading needs of the blind. But it doesn't, any more than the cane and dog get people where they are going. No matter how many devices and strategies I use, I still run into situations where I need to read and can't. There is no perfect substitute for vision.

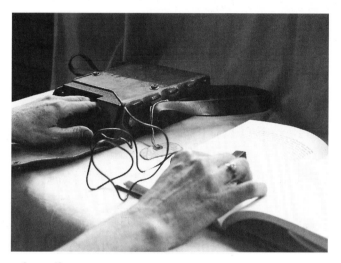

An opticon

how do you WRITE?

Close your eyes and try signing your name. Maybe the signature doesn't look too bad. Now close your eyes again and try writing a few sentences. That's more complicated. Did you write words on top of different words? Did you angle across the page, covering up whole sentences?

When I lost my sight, I made all those mistakes and more. So I typed. In high school, I'd taken a class, learning to type by feel, not by sight. Frankly, I hated the boring drills, memorizing the keyboard, but when I lost my sight, I was grateful. Unlike most of the other newly blind adults in the training program, I still had a way to communicate with the outside world.

Not that my typing was perfect. I made mistakes. Once I typed a letter to a friend and had accidentally pressed the stencil key (before copy machines, this key struck the letters without using ink, for a mimeograph machine). That resulted in two blank pages arriving at her apartment in California.

The training program sharpened my typing skills, so that I made fewer mistakes and never sent out another blank letter. The program also offered a handwriting class. Many people who are born blind never learn to write more than their own names. Forming letters, connecting them, crossing *t*'s, dotting *i*'s is very visual. When you wrote with your eyes closed, your handwriting probably

This is a handwriting guide. It helps you to write in straight lines. If you are visually impaired, it is very helpful for writing letters

48

looked about the same as it always does. Over time, a blind person's handwriting deteriorates from lack of practice and from not being able to check it with her eyes. I don't use a pencil very much: it now feels odd in my hand. Still, I try to write with one occasionally, making grocery lists or notes to my husband using a handwriting guide.

The Braille writer has only nine keys. Six of them are for making the six Braille dots. As you push down on the keys, the machine strikes the back of the paper, raising dots that correspond to letters, numbers, or punctuation on the front side. Two keys are for moving backward and forward. The last key moves the paper out of the machine.

In the training program I also learned to write with a Braille writer and slate and stylus. With these four strategies I managed the mechanics of writing, but it didn't occur to me to try creative writing until much later.

Of course, I'd done some writing before I was blind. In junior high and high school, two friends and I wrote songs—terrible, tasteless things. After one of my friends' mother tape-recorded our songs, and we listened—and actually thought we had potential—we began to take ourselves more seriously. Our songs probably didn't improve, but we took more time with them.

A high school English teacher told me I had a knack for writing. After that, I paid more attention to my essays, revising them more often, trying to use original, fresh details.

Yet a sequence of events had to take place before I thought about a writing career. First, I went blind and became a reader. Second, I wanted to read to my kids. But with illustrated Braille children's books so scarce, I was forced to tell them stories I remembered. When I'd exhausted all the stories I knew, I made up my own. Finally, I heard about a writ-

49

Babar in twin vision (print and pictures, and Braille)

ing group in a local children's bookstore. I joined, put my stories down on paper, and within a year was hooked. At first, I wrote talking animal books about excessively tall giraffes or hippos that wouldn't cuddle, but soon I wrote from the heart, books I needed to write—books about my own life.

I wrote my first two children's books on an ancient typewriter. I considered using a Braille writer or dictation machine to have feedback the typewriter didn't provide, but, for some reason, my words flowed more smoothly on the typewriter than on those machines. I typed quickly and accurately, but faced a lot of frustrations.

More than once, the paper fell to the floor without my knowing right away, and I kept typing. I only discovered my mistake when I touched the roller and found it empty. Although I scrambled to recreate what I'd written, I probably never got it exactly the same.

I had to wait until my husband, kids, or readers came to read the draft of the story into a tape recorder. Then I listened and took Braille notes for any corrections I wanted to make. After that, I returned to the typewriter and rewrote the whole book. The tedious process started over again: type, wait, listen, rewrite.

At times I thought of quitting. Besides the challenges my blindness presented, I faced rejection, and that was disappointing. Writing is one thing, and actually getting a book published is completely different. That's why I decided I needed a literary agent to help sell my work.

Just before I sold my first book, I resolved to give myself two more years to publish. Many people didn't publish books, I reminded myself, and they had perfectly happy lives. Maybe there was another career I'd be better at.

Two months later I sold a book. When my agent phoned to tell me, I couldn't stop jumping up and down. I called my husband immediately, and he just yelled over and over again, "All right!" When my kids came home from school, we hopped a bus to meet my husband for a fancy dinner.

After I sold another book, I bought a computer. It's an everyday computer with one different feature—talking software, which makes the computer speak every word I type. If I type c-a-t and hit the space bar, the computer says the whole word, *cat.* Another keystroke makes the computer read the whole sentence. Another makes it read a paragraph, and still another, the entire document.

If I spell a word wrong, c-t-a for *cat*, for example, the computer spells the word out loud. That way I can correct my typos.

When I was downstairs one day, I heard the computer on the second floor speaking, and I knew I hadn't even turned it on. It was making mistakes that I hadn't had anything to do with. I went to the stairs to listen. The computer wasn't just speaking; it was swearing.

I took the stairs two at a time and found my son and his friends around the machine, typing in one bad word after another.

Since then, I've had no other funny surprises from the computer, just annoying breakdowns. These mishaps remind me how much I rely on the computer.

my writing group

Sally's writing group friends

Along with all the sophisticated technology, I also rely on a low-tech secret weapon: my writing group. Each week we read and critique manuscripts and catch up on each other's lives. Twice a month I lead another group, where I hear and critique manuscripts. Some say the writing life is solitary, but regular workshops provide contact with people able to give intelligent criticism and close friendship.

One of Sally's closest friends, children's book author Colleen O'Shaughnessy McKenna

more tools for writing

CHECK-WRITING STENCIL

Many blindness agencies produce check-writing stencils designed to match personal checks. Usually the stencil consists of two pieces of cardboard or plastic the size of the check, hinged together at one end. You slide the check inside and fill in the cut-out slots with the date, recipient, amount, and signature.

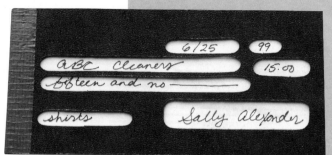

THE SLATE AND STYLUS

The slate is made up of two rectangular pieces of aluminum or plastic hinged together at one end. The front piece usually has four lines of eighteen to twenty-seven cut-out Braille cells. Each cell has three grooves on either side, corresponding to the six Braille dots. The stylus, a punching device about two inches long, fits into the grooves to make the dots. When paper is inside the slate, you place the stylus in the cut-out cell farthest to the right and begin punching in the correct dots.

The slate and stylus are cheaper and more portable than the Braille writer. But they are harder to use. Because you punch down with the stylus, the dots come out on the back side of the paper. So you have to write from right to left and make every letter backward. The Braille writer pushes up the dots from the back to the front side of the paper, so you write every letter the same way you read it.

when you lost your sight, did you seek out blind FRIENDS?

question ten

One time when I called my brother's office, I spoke to his assistant. "Bobby's out of town, but I'll have him call you tomorrow," he said. "I know he has two sisters, and I've met one of you."

"I'm the charming one," I said, joking.

"Well then, it's you I've met," he said, "because the other sister is blind."

As shocked as I was by his comment, I could easily have thought the same thing when I was sighted. The blind aren't usually considered charming. Scary, maybe, or helpless or pitiful, but definitely not charming.

After I became blind, many of my parents' friends expected me to surround myself instantly with blind people. They assumed that any dates I had would have visual problems, like me. Just recently, I had my piano tuned by a blind man. After he'd left, I went out to mail a letter. A house painter on our street stopped me to ask, "Was that your husband who just walked by?"

I'm not sure why his assumption bothered me. I think I felt robbed of my identity. I was blind, so I wasn't as much a person as I was a member of a group. Who said I wanted to be in this group anyway?

The truth was that, at first, I didn't—partly because of the negative image of the blind, and partly because I already had a group of extra-

54

Sally and Pam Nutter Lauderback, 1968

ordinary sighted friends. My roommates, Pam and Maria; my best friend from college, Carol; and many others supported me through my blindness.

Yet I faced a geographic problem—these close friends were scattered all over the country. I was heading for Pittsburgh to begin a training program for blind adults, and I'd need to find friends there.

That spring I became one of thirty-three students in the program, and despite my resistance to making blind friends, I realized these friendships were inevitable and important. All of us shared the frustration of learning to function in a different way.

After graduation, I had a three-week break before returning to the training program as a staff member. At this time I learned that my best friend in the program had died from diabetes. He was from Pittsburgh, and although we wouldn't have worked together, I'd counted on him for general support.

Work kept me too busy to dwell on my loss. As the weeks passed, lunch with other staff members turned into invitations for dinner. Soon my free time was filled by a nice circle of friends from work, all sighted. I was the only blind person on the staff.

In a year I entered graduate school to study

Sally and Carol Patterson, 1968. Carol visited Sally every day in the hospital.

social work. I made more friends there, but they were also people who could see. Most were thoughtful and sensitive, I figured from studying psychology and communications, and they seemed at ease with me as I thumped around the classroom buildings with my cane.

But soon I began to long for blind friends. I wanted to share everyday annoyances that came from being blind; talk to them about different problems, such as the issue of give and take. I'd never kept a tally of favors before I was blind, but now I did. I didn't want to accept more help than I gave, because friends might feel burdened or cheated. I needed to talk to other blind people and find out if they had the same concerns.

So I decided to reach out. I called a blind social worker I'd heard about and invited her to dinner. I met another blind graduate student and got to know him. These two friends were a comfort. Right away I brought up some problems.

Sally and Maria Nutera, 1968

We talked about finding people to help us shop for clothes, the confusing elevator system at the university, the finger-eating revolving doors, the job market.

Over the years, I've developed more blind friendships. Some friends have influenced me politically: just as there is a civil rights movement, there is a movement for the rights of the disabled, and I'm active in it. Others fill me in on where I can buy aids and appliances, or just talk to me about everyday things.

Still, after all these years of being blind, my best friends are sighted. My husband, kids, other family members, and the writers in my weekly group are my most constant companions. My husband takes me to plays, dance clubs, and concerts, and has challenged me to enter running events (holding his arm) and bike races (on a two-seater). I've challenged him to water ski and do a rope course with me. My kids know how much I value physical exercise. Leslie got me involved in aerobics, and Joel is determined that I shall connect regularly with a golf ball.

And I look forward to other adventures. A commercial pilot and I might go gliding. I'll be the one in control. He says that I'll be able to feel the thermal air currents and hear the audio variometer signaling ups and downs to avoid

Bob and Sally on the tandem bike

objects. Does that sound crazy? Maybe. But I'll probably try it, especially since the pilot will be along to tell me left and right turns and to take over before we land.

tales of
bravery
and
accomplishment

Blind adventurer Bill Irwin (right) and his dog guide hiked the Appalachian Trail alone and survived a three-day snowstorm in a ranger cabin.

A Navajo man, blinded in Vietnam, makes wonderful sculptures, despite the loss of three fingers and his sight.

A woman, blind from a motorcycle accident, still cross-country skis, rides horseback, teaches her horse to do stunts, and does all the lambing when her sheep give birth.

Another blind woman does woodwork that rivals anything produced by sighted artists. Several blind people even paint landscapes fine enough to be shown in galleries.

Blind athletes have won Special Olympic medals for downhill ski races.

Recently, a man set the record for being the only blind man—and the oldest person—to swim across the Hudson River.

do people treat you DIFFERENTLY?

Once while I waited at a bus stop, a man took my arm and began tugging me across the street. "What are you doing?" I asked. The man wouldn't answer. He obviously wanted to help me through the intersection.

"I'm waiting for a bus," I told him. "I don't want to cross this street."

"Oh, sorry," he finally muttered and led me back to the stop.

After I lost my sight, I encountered this kind of strange reaction now and then. Not from everyone, of course. There have always been sensitive people who have been completely comfortable with me.

But some people do treat me differently. A few make me feel labeled and stereotyped, especially those who've never come into contact with the blind before. I've met people who expect me to know every blind person in the world, people who assume I'm depressed all the time, and others who see me as a saint who'd never take a sip of wine or use the tamest swear word. Many seem surprised that I have a sense of humor.

Even professors haven't known how to treat me. Right after I left the Greater Pittsburgh Guild for the Blind, I started graduate school. Each semester it would be up to me to find all the Braille and recorded materials for my courses. When exams came, none of my professors knew how I'd be able to take exams. So I made a suggestion: I would bring a typewriter and reader, if they would find me an empty room. But they never did. So I ended up taking exams in the ladies' bathroom, trying to ignore the flushing toilets and conversations.

Usually, people who aren't used to being with the blind want to help but don't know how. That was the case with the man who dragged me across the street. His intentions were good, but he was too uncomfortable even to ask me what I needed.

Others make different mistakes. For example, some waiters act as if I'm deaf, as well as blind.

"What does she want?" they ask my sighted friend.

Even though I always order for myself, some waiters still speak to the person I'm sitting with, not to me. I wonder if it's because they can't make eye contact with me and can't tell if they have my attention.

Store clerks have done the same thing. After one had asked my friend three questions about me, all of which I'd answered, she then asked a fourth, "Will she pay by check or cash?"

That's when I lost my temper. "Ask me! I can't see, but I can hear every word you're saying."

I know I embarrassed the woman, but she'd treated me as if I were invisible, and that made me furious. Being invisible meant being left out, ignored, made to feel less important than my friend who wasn't even the customer. Being invisible also meant something else. I couldn't see this clerk. Maybe she couldn't see me. Had I disappeared? Of course not, but her treatment gave me the sensation that I'd lost myself, lost my identity.

As annoying as these little incidents are, other situations are truly painful. One of the worst was when I gave birth to my son. At the time, most new mothers were permitted to have their babies in the room with them all day, but for me it was different. The head nurse wouldn't allow it. "He might turn blue or stop breathing," she said, "and you wouldn't know it."

I was crushed. Imagine my knowing that all the other new mothers had their babies in their arms, as I sat alone without mine.

By the end of the first day, the floor nurses had watched me feed and handle him. Despite the head nurse's rule, they sneaked him in.

When my daughter was born, the same thing happened, even though I now had experience. This time I offered to sign a form releasing the hospital of responsibility in case something did happen. Still, the head nurse refused. I buried my face in the pillow and cried.

Sally, Bob, and Joel, 1976

Once again, the nurses saw how competent I was and sneaked the baby right in. I held Leslie the whole time, feeling her heart beating against me, enjoying her compact little body, her wonderful smell, her sounds.

When I could see, I never felt mistreated by people I met in public. But after becoming blind, I did. Now I was a member of a minority.

In graduate school I met lots of minority students. Like me, they often didn't feel accepted as equals, and often they felt stereotyped. "I'm supposed to be athletic, not smart," an African-American student told me, "just the way you're supposed to be depressed and helpless." Yet at the same time, in graduate school and other places, people showed acceptance, and sometimes even curiosity and awareness.

Two Lions' Clubs that raised money for the blind asked me to speak about how I'd adjusted to losing my sight. A few months later, a Rotary

Club asked me to talk. Soon, I was giving speeches every three months about blindness.

Then, I decided to turn one of these talks into an article—to be read instead of heard—and a newspaper published it. I wrote another for my college alumni magazine.

Without intending to, I became a spokesperson for the blind. Eventually, I began writing about my experiences in books for children.

I suppose that if people hadn't treated me differently in ways I disliked, I probably wouldn't have had so much I wanted to say. I probably wouldn't have begun to give talks and to write. Maybe then, for me, mistreatment led to something good.

Sally visiting a class at Emerson Elementary School, Parkersburg, West Virginia

The day I became totally blind divided my life into two parts, before and after. I felt trapped at first, as if someone had thrown a blanket over my head, and I wanted to get out. I yearned to scream, *I'm inside. Doesn't anybody out there see that? Doesn't anybody remember me?* I thought I was still the same person.

has being blind CHANGED you?

question twelve

But of course, I wasn't the same and never would be again. Blindness was responsible for a whole new life for me, and even though I learned the skills necessary to make me independent again, I could never be the same.

Now, thirty years later, am I completely different? Almost, but those who knew me before still see plenty of the old me sneaking out.

Before my vision deteriorated, I wasn't a religious person, but the threat of going blind scared me a lot. Enough, in fact, that I began to pray. At twenty-five years old, I prayed like a child. "Please, God, don't let this happen." I bargained, "Just one eye." Soon my prayers expanded to include my family, friends, everyone I met at the hospital.

But because of what was happening to me, my mother stopped going to church, and my fiancé stopped believing in God. Other friends offered religious explanations.

"God is taking away your sight because you are strong," they said, or, "You did something wrong, and God is punishing you."

I just couldn't accept that God was the cause, that God was punishing me. I believed that my blindness came from some unexplained disease, not from God. So I continued my praying, not really because I

63

expected a cure, but because afterward I felt calmer and more peaceful. These times of quiet meditation and prayer helped me develop the strength I needed to adjust to my new life. Many people don't need religion to face their difficulties, but since becoming blind, I do.

Growing up, I was an outgoing, very talkative person. Right after I lost my sight, however, I overheard my aunt say, "Sally's grown so quiet."

I had to quiet down. Without sight, my ears became a lifeline to other human beings. Blindness took away the nonverbal clues that showed people's fatigue, sadness, joy, or concern. I learned to listen well and began picking up those emotions in their voices.

Before my blindness, I relied—as most people do—almost exclusively on sight. Now I pay attention to my remaining senses.

For example, my sense of touch: feeling an empty ice cube tray in the freezer of my refrigerator is a sure sign that my son is home.

Or my sense of smell: smelling eggs cooking tells me he is awake.

Or my sense of hearing: I used to play piano with sheet music. Now I play by ear. My father was a jazz pianist who never had to read a note of music. Growing up, I used to plunk out the melody with two fingers at the top of the keyboard, while he played George Gershwin or Cole Porter on the bottom. When I

Sally at the piano

64

became blind, I discovered that I had his ear. Now I play piano most days and love it.

In addition to giving information, my nonvisual senses give pleasure. This year I planted a scented garden full of lavender, lemon balm, and day lilies. I don't need daylight for weeding and clipping and planting. People often find me among my shasta daisies after dark. Sometimes I think the blind have a secret advantage. We tune into another part of the surrounding world, to birdsongs and textures and fragrances often ignored.

Sally in her garden with Ursula

But at what cost? I can seldom relax while doing ordinary things. I concentrate all day long, from the moment my feet hit the bedroom floor. I've memorized the layout of my home so I don't need a cane or a dog to guide me. Yet I have to know if I'm on carpet or tile or hardwood to keep my bearings. I step cautiously, because a misplaced chair or shoe could trip me. No longer can I pop into a car and race off to the park. I walk there step by step with my dog, listening to every vehicle that passes, heeding every auditory and tactual clue. Still, when I sit at the computer or cook dinner, I forget that I'm blind. This may sound strange, but really it is a blessing. Who would want to dwell on her disability every moment of the day?

Blindness has changed me into a new person. It's not only taken away my sight, but a teaching career I loved, and many recreational activities, especially sports. But it has given me so much. If by some magic I were able to see again, I would try not to give up the joys of smelling and touching and tasting and hearing. I wouldn't give up being a writer, a reader, a waterskier, or a listener. My life is not easier this way, but it is definitely better.

Sally with her third grade class, Valencia School, Brea, California, 1967, six months before her vision began deteriorating

do you remember the color BLUE?

question thirteen

Because I could see for twenty-six years, I can remember the color blue. Say the word, and I picture robins' eggs, bluebirds, forget-me-nots, and cornflowers. My mind sees sapphire, turquoise, azure, and navy.

Since I became blind, my visual memory has faded. Like all human beings, I've lost brain cells—about one thousand a day after turning forty, in fact. Scary, until you realize that I had ten billion at my peak, around the age of seventeen or eighteen. Also, the part of the brain that is used for seeing is not being stimulated because of the damage to my retinas. Those brain cells are dying, too.

I do use my imagination to see things. This habit of forming mental pictures helps me hang on to my visual memory. It's the reason my memory has only faded and not disappeared totally.

I still dream in full-color pictures, but my dreams contain as many sensations of touch, smell, sound, and taste as of sight. For the first few months after I lost my vision, I would wake up from a technicolor moving picture dream and feel shocked at not being able to see.

67

One minute I was driving my baby blue Volkswagen Beetle along a California freeway. The next minute I woke up and saw mist.

People who are born blind, the congenitally blind, can't see pictures or colors in their minds. Many sighted people explain that blue looks cool or cozy or sad. Red is hot and exciting. Yellow is bright and cheerful. These descriptions don't work. Having never seen, congenitally blind people can't form a concept of color, dark or light, stripes, checks, or polka dots.

Even though I can form color images in my mind, what I imagine isn't exactly like the real thing.

When I could still see, my psychology professor once asked our class to do an experiment on sensory deprivation. He blindfolded us and took us around a room. While my teacher gave a description of the chairs, lamps, walls, and carpet, I touched everything. Based on that information, I tried to paint a picture in my mind of what the room looked like. When I took the blindfold off, I was amazed. The room seemed shrunken. It wasn't nearly as wide or big as I'd imagined. The furniture, carpet, and walls were in completely different shades.

Joel Alexander, 1997

Although my visualizing isn't perfect, my visual memory adds richness to my life. Sometimes people describe my kids as looking like a certain movie star or famous person I can remember seeing. My son is supposed to look like an old movie actor, Victor Mature, for instance. Since I remember the

68

actor perfectly, that information has helped me to form a more accurate portrait. My sister and brother will tell me that my kids resemble a certain photo of me at a particular age. That helps too. Of course, my husband claims to look exceedingly like Robert Redford, but that just makes me laugh.

Have you ever gotten to know somebody's voice on the telephone or radio and later met him? Did he look different from the way you visualized him? Choose a partner and try this experiment. Close your eyes while your partner finds a picture of someone in a magazine. Have the friend describe the person to you. Imagine what he looks like. Then open your eyes and look at the photo. Did you picture the person you see in front of you?

Above: Sally, age 7
Below: Leslie, age 9

Close your eyes again and picture the color blue. How many different shades can you remember?

I can't think of the color blue without going back in time to Greenwood, a small lake with a beach and sandy bottom, surrounded by woods. I learned to fish and swim at Greenwood and found lasting friends there. Today, my family and I still vacation in a big bungalow on the water. I can picture the lake all year long, changing color throughout the day, throughout the season. At times, it's a great shimmering aquamarine, then royal blue or turquoise or sapphire. All the shades are perfect, and so is Greenwood. Today when I hear water lapping against the shore, feel sand gripping my feet, smell the woods, experience Greenwood in a close-up, intense way, I'm immediately taken back to my past. The vivid blue of the lake in all its hues fills my mind, and I remember an easier time. The two parts of my life, my past and present, the carefree and complex, unite, and I'm conscious of how rich and good life is.

Bob, Sally, and Leslie at Greenwood Lake

what does it feel like to be blind?
try your own training program

close your eyes:

1. Go into your closet and touch different clothes. Can you identify them just from your fingertips? Clothes with unusual buttons, pockets, zippers, frills, or bows are easy to identify. But different-colored T-shirts and jeans feel the same. You could end up wearing a wild outfit—red jeans with an orange-striped shirt. To distinguish among T-shirts, jeans, and other problem clothes, I pin medal Braille tags onto the inside labels.

2. Take a seat at the dinner table. Curl your fingertips so you won't knock over your glass, and trail your hand along either side of your plate to locate your utensils and drink. Now touch the food on your plate with a fork. Can you identify the meat just by your sense of touch? The vegetables? The potatoes? Sometimes people help a blind person to locate his food by pretending that the dinner plate is the face of a clock. They say that the meat is at six o'clock or three o'clock, wherever it is positioned on the plate. Can you cut your meat? Pork and lamb chops and other meat with bones are difficult to cut.

3. Go into your bathroom and try to figure out which bottles are the shampoo, the conditioner, the mousse, and the gel. Does your sense of touch help? Your sense of smell? Would you need to buy these products in differently shaped containers? Can you blow-dry your hair without peeking? What about makeup? I put on lipstick by feel. I rub blush in five times per cheek. Can you imagine putting on eye liner and mascara without poking your eye? But I manage it.

4. Stand beside your parents as they cook. Do you hear the water rumble to know it's boiling? Can you hear butter sizzling in the pan?

5. Try walking through your bedroom without bumping into anything. Would you have to keep the room neater if you couldn't see?

6. Punch in your best friend's telephone number. Did you hit the right keys?

7. Feel a quarter and a nickel. They aren't exactly the same size. Now feel the edges. One is rough, and one is smooth. Which is which? Now feel a dime and penny. They are nearly the same size, but the edges are different. Which coin has the rough edge? Unlike coins, bills all feel the same, so somebody sighted has to tell me the denominations. Then I fold each of them differently—fives in half, tens in fourths, and twenties in thirds. I don't fold my ones at all.

a note about blindness

Sally Hobart Alexander lost her vision between the ages of twenty-four and twenty-six. Her story is not a common one, and is not representative of how most people lose their vision—although many people, and especially children, fear that they may start to go blind as suddenly as Sally did. This is very unlikely, although it is what we commonly see in movies and on television. This is probably one reason why blindness is so feared and misunderstood.

Not all blind people lose their vision completely. While some people, like Sally, retain no useful vision, some lose only their central vision and their ability to read while retaining peripheral sight and their ability to get around. Others who lose their peripheral vision may have difficulty walking around safely, but they may be able to read normal print through small tunnels of vision in the centers of their retinas.

One thing that all people with visual impairments experience, however, is social situations where people respond to them awkwardly or inappropriately. In *Do You Remember the Color Blue?* Sally Hobart Alexander shares the feelings she has experienced about ways she has been treated over the years—explaining as she says in chapter one, that "losing your vision isn't just one loss, it's many."

Richard L. Welsh, Ph.D.
President
Pittsburgh Vision Services

resources

If you are interested in knowing more about blindness or volunteering to help people with visual impairments, you can contact one of the following organizations:

For information:

Lighthouse International
111 East 59th Street, 12th Floor
New York, NY 10022-1202

American Foundation for the Blind
11 Pennsylvania Plaza, Suite 300
New York, NY 10001

American Council of the Blind
1155 15th Street, NW, Suite 720
Washington, DC 20005

Braille Institute
(Southern California)
1-800-BRAILLE (272-4553).

Pittsburgh Vision Services
http://www.pghvis.org

To volunteer:

Reading for the Blind and Dyslexic
5022 Hollywood Boulevard
Los Angeles, CA 90027

Guide Dogs for the Blind, Inc.
P.O. Box 151200
San Rafael, California 94915-1200
1-800-295-4050
http://www.guidedogs.com

acknowledgments

In creating this book, I owe much to many and give special thanks to:

Jill Davis, my wise, candid, positive, demanding editor; and associate editor, Judy Carey, who was able to see the butterfly in my caterpillar draft, and who joined Jill in teaching and encouraging me;

Kendra Marcus, my agent, counselor, playmate;

Bob Alexander, for tedious proofreading and for endless pursuit of photos and equally endless mailings to Viking, i.e., to the avaricious Jill;

Leslie Alexander, for hours in search of the right photos, and when none turned up, for taking excellent shots, and as always for detecting schmaltz in my writing;

Joel Alexander, for modeling services;

Richard Welsh, Ph.D., director of the Pittsburgh Vision Services, for his concluding remarks in the book and all his many kindnesses;

Dr. Richard Bowers, opthamologist and encyclopedia of information on the eye, for being so available and eager to teach;

Ralph Tartar, Ph.D., neuropsychologist, who, like Richard, was available, thoroughly informed, and willing to explain;

Three thousand cheers to my writing group, Nancy, Kathy, Dick, Patty, and Colleen;

Colleen O'Shaughnessy McKenna, prolific children's author, friend as close as a sister, who sorted through my disorganized photo albums and pretended to enjoy it;

Kathy Ayres, children's author and terrific friend who makes house calls for garden, home, and photography emergencies;

Carol Woolman, dear college friend and amateur photographer, whose photos appear in the book;

Bob and Barb Hobart, my brother and sister-in-law, who energetically dug through their photographic archives;

Bob and Kate Hobart and Ruth and Fred Alexander, now deceased, who took many of these photographs, without knowing the wide audience that would view them;

George Ancona, my family's favorite photographer, who worked miracles even without computer technology;

Jason Feldstein and Eric Lasky, my dutiful readers;

Karen Good, Information Service Coordinator, Pittsburgh Vision Services;

Dr. Richard Kavner, optometrist;

Nina Putignano, assistant art director at Viking, for designing the book;

Bruce Katz, for photographing the tools and gadgets;

Morey Waltuck, for valuable input;

Rosemary Gerrity and the Western Pennsylvania School for the Deaf;

Lois Meadows, Matthew Lasky, Sandy Evans;

Valencia Elementary School third graders, 1967;

Julie Lane at the Lighthouse for the Blind, New York City, for generously supplying equipment for photographs;

The Pittsburgh Vision Services, (formerly two agencies: The Greater Pittsburgh Guild for the Blind and the Pittsburgh Blind Association), for offering crucial pictures;

Pete Jackson of The Seeing Eye, and Bill Irwin;

The American Foundation for the Blind, New York City, for research data.

index